LAUREN FORD'S CHRISTMAS BOOK

Books by Lauren Ford

THE LITTLE BOOK ABOUT GOD

THE AGELESS STORY

OUR LADY'S BOOK

LAUREN FORD'S CHRISTMAS BOOK

LAUREN FORD'S CHRISTMAS BOOK

Text and Pictures by
LAUREN FORD

Scripture from
the Gospel of St. Luke

DODD, MEAD & COMPANY

NEW YORK

To Samuel Golden and Dorothy Bryan,
who both wanted this book to be realized.

Copyright © 1963 by Lauren Ford

Library of Congress Catalog Card Number: 63-18780
Printed in the United States of America

THE COMING OF CHRIST

I have been asked to tell the story of Christmas in my own way and I should love to because it is the most wonderful story there is, but I should much rather leave the main telling to Saint Luke and I shall ramble on with the thoughts that run through my mind as I make the pictures.

Gospel of St. Luke

CHAPTER 2, VERSES 1 THROUGH 20

And it came to pass that in those days there went out a decree from Caesar Augustus, that the whole world should be enrolled.

I have chosen St. Luke because his telling is inimitable. One never tires of hearing it. Every time, we find something new to marvel at. Each evangelist who wrote of the birth of Christ took up a different aspect of it, according to his own individual personality. Any true event, being rich and full, will touch off

in each human being that which triggers
his own personal enthusiasm.

St. Luke was an artist. He was a
sensitive apparatus, so the events were
recorded by him as a series of pictures,
as a taping of sounds. His need was to
document these inspiring events, as they
had stimulated his own creative being.

This enrolling was first made by Cyrinus, the governor of Syria.

And all went to be enrolled, every one into his own city.

The prophets had prophesied to the Jewish people, the instructors had instructed them that they were to expect a King, a great ruler who was to take the place of all those domineering Roman potentates who did not understand the Hebrew feelings and culture. That was the whole trouble.

It was the manner of Christ's coming that took all of Israel so greatly by surprise. The people were accustomed to rulers who came in pomp and purple-satin glory. It was the humble circumstances that proved too much for them to take, except for the shepherds. Simple shepherds, accustomed to the grandeur of the night, to them the angels showed their more than earthly glory.

And Joseph also went up from Galilee, out of the city of Nazareth into Judea, to the city of David, which is called Bethlehem, because he was of the house and family of David.

To be enrolled with Mary his espoused wife, who was with child.

Among these an angel was suddenly standing, announcing the coming of Christ, the Saviour of the world, in a poor little stable—also familiar to them.

"Do not be afraid; behold, I bring you good news of a great rejoicing for the whole people. This day, in the city of David, a Saviour has been born for you, the Lord Christ Himself. This is the sign by which you are to know Him; you will find a Child still in swaddling clothes, lying in a manger."

And it came to pass, that when they were there, her days were accomplished, that she should be delivered.

And she brought forth her first-born son, and wrapped him up in swaddling clothes, and laid him in a manger, because there was no room for them in the inn.

These humble circumstances have been particularly devised to touch us all.

Suddenly, there was with the angel a multitude of angels saying, "Glory to God in high heaven and peace on earth to men that are God's friends."

And there were in the same country shepherds watching, and keeping the night-watches over their flock.

And behold an angel of the Lord stood by them, and the brightness of God shone round about them, and they feared with a great fear.

The angels were announcing the coming of Him Who spoke of peace all through His life. "Peace be unto you," He offers over and over.

Even during that last meal, on the night He was to be "lifted up," which must have been the customary way of saying crucified—even then He was telling His followers clearly what was to take place. His own twelve—His chosen ones—did not understand Him.

*And the angel said to them: Fear not; for, behold, I bring
you good tidings of great joy, that shall be to all the people;*

For this day is born to you a Saviour, who is Christ the Lord,
in the city of David.

But "Peace," He said, "My Peace I leave you—My peace I give unto you. Not as the world gives, give I unto you." This was His Christmas gift—that "Peace which the world cannot give." It is not a peace from one nation to another, but an inner peace. This He gives us. All we need is to want it.

The Inns of Bethlehem were noisy places, full of camels, ponies, donkeys, and other animals in a great open yard, where the people could unroll their own bedding and water and feed their beasts and themselves. Or they could retire for a few minutes into the sheds that surrounded the court, safe from the brigands of the open road. Not a very private place for our tiny Son of God to be born.

And this shall be a sign unto you: You shall find the infant wrapped in swaddling clothes, and laid in a manger.

And suddenly there was with the angel a multitude of the heavenly army, praising God, and saying:

The old Bethlehem is up the hill a little farther than the present town, where caves in the hillsides—some wood fronted, with heavy doors to cosy-in the little beasts—are still in use, in exactly the same way, even today. Here our little Baby King was born.

It was near here that the angel stood among the shepherds, giving the directions that showed them where to look for the Child.

Glory to God in the highest; and on earth peace to men of good will.

And here the shepherds came and found the Baby and Mary and Joseph and the little beasts, all as the angel had told them, and they knew that this was the Christ.

It was here, too, still in Bethlehem, that the Wise Men came from the East and found the young Child, after their stopover with Herod. This is interesting because we know that astrologists and astronomers were numerous in the East at that time, and if a special star were to appear, it would be natural for them to follow that star.

And it came to pass, after the angels departed from them into heaven, the shepherds said one to another: Let us go over to Bethlehem and let us see this word that is come to pass, which the Lord hath shewed to us.

And they came with haste; and they found Mary and Joseph, and the infant lying in the manger.

And because of the prophesies and their knowledge of history, they knew that the star would show at the time when the promised King was to be born. So they came and found the Babe and paid their respects and gave Him their presents of gold, frankincense and myrrh.

And seeing, they understood of the word that had been spoken to them concerning this child.

And all that heard, wondered: and at those things that were told them by the shepherds.

Then they went off, leaving Mary and Joseph and the Babe to follow their lives in the way that we all know, until that Child had given us His wisdom, His love, and His life and, through His Resurrection, His proof of Immortality.

But Mary kept all these words, pondering them in her heart.
And the shepherds returned, glorifying and praising God,
for all the things they had heard and seen, as it was told unto
them.

Lauren Ford

outstanding American artist, was born in New York City. Her mother was Julia Ellsworth Ford, the author of many books and plays for children, and her father, the late Simeon Ford, owner of the Grand Union Hotel, was a famous wit, and a popular public speaker. Her mother is the authority for the statement that Lauren Ford began to draw at the age of four. She studied art with George Bridgman and Frank V. du Mond. She is represented in such distinguished galleries as the Metropolitan Museum of Art in New York, the Corcoran Gallery of Art in Washington, D. C., and the Art Institute of Chicago, as well as among the treasures of discriminating private collectors.

For all her great success, Lauren Ford prefers to live a simple, independent life on her working farm near Bethlehem, Connecticut, surrounded by her family and friends, a continual procession of interesting guests from all over the world, and the farm animals which often serve as her models—as does the gracious Connecticut countryside that she loves so well. She paints at all times and places, most often pictures of a religious nature. Her exquisite Christmas cards are treasured throughout the year by their delighted recipients. The Nativity scene is frequently pictured in her own barn, with her good farm neighbors gathered about the Manger. Their dogs and cats come along, too!

Life Magazine has twice featured the art of Lauren Ford, and her work has been the subject of much favorable comment from competent critics, who describe it as "picturesque," "fanciful" and "tender."